# Days of Xmas Poems

## A. Razor

Punk ☆ Hostage ☆ Press

**Day of Xmas Poems**
A. Razor

© A. Razor

ISBN-13: 978-1505302813
ISBN-10: 1505302811

Punk Hostage Press
p.o. box 1869
Hollywood CA
90078
www.punkhostagepress.com
@punkhostage

Cover Design – A. Razor

Co-opted Cover Artwork – Winston Smith

**Intro-**

Tis' the season...being born on December 25th can give you a little insight into the biggest shopping holiday in the world. The insight is never a complete overview of anything at all, other than all the things a child gets sold on that wash away into lost dreams for the adult. There is the religious and the agnostic approaches, there is the atheist experience of self, inside of a world turned inside out over the rhetoric of fantastical tales from yore. Then there is the heartbreak side, the coal in the stocking, the overworked and underpaid that Dickens couldn't save. I melted it all down and smeared it inside my skull for the world to see. Merry Xmas and all that comes with another winter wonderland of splendor before us now.

A. Razor, December 2014

*"we rode wild as children who had been orphaned by all the doom"* – a. razor

БГОАВЛЕНИЕ ГДНЕ

ІС҃ ХС҃.

## A Seasonal Riff off of T.S. Eliot's –
## 'The Cultivation of Christmas Trees'

there is a time of year happening now, always
now
child-like candle lights become stars up high

       there are sounds people make, some
joyous/some sorrowful
these songs they sing are all nostalgia for a
time before this, a time
   without plastic or inoculation, a time of
tempest unknown, weather
     left uncharted, wars fought without
regard or warning or

        public debate
a time of cultivation that was inadequate &
wasteful, a time of
   trees that were not seen as a vanishing
resource, but never forgotten
   as a form of spiritual reliquary that were
worshiped w/ fire

not much has been saved, how could it be
saved?  what we had__needed to be
   used up for growth, for progress toward
capital, for refinement of all things
    for the sake of all that had come before us,
hoping for a second

        coming
that might set the record straight, once and
for all

you see, the sacrifice was

necessary, regardless, it was made
                                        so the stories we
listen to now, by dwindling
                          flames of sufficient
force to light the cumbersome way
                    these are the stories that were
seeded & cared for, all those years
        of prosperous yule ago, when a wink
might have meant more than the
exclamation of 'holiday sale' means today, as
we starve for attention, not
noticing the dwindling supply of feast for the
heart & the soul as well

        we dream of saviors

who might be born

                into our world now

    but, like christmas

            trees, cut down too soon

        to ever be known to us

                        in time

## On the 1st Day of Xmas

On the First Day of Xmas
there was a frost all over
even the tropics felt it
as December turned
on the cold axis alone
leaving all odd numbered years
to find sanctuary in getting even
with all the clouded horizons
coming head on to tell all the fortune
before the new year begins

## On the 2<sup>nd</sup> Day of Xmas

you just want to be loved, without the whisky-
--this here
is the lament of burned up Xmas trees past

two days away from barstow, is how love gets
remembered
dead somewhere in a ditch out in the desert,
forsaken__for certain

a long beaded brow shows no remorse or
contempt, just working
too hard for the daydream to survive another
nightmare---walking

we head away somewhere, on the back of a
bus, trying to save...
something or just someone---can't ever
remember that part correctly

the shoes wear out, more than the soles, more
than the soul---a foot
at a time until we make it back to where the
pine cones are found

lying about upon the ground, scored by winds
of time, seeds of change
brought forth by trial---by fire...by the by,
along the way as it is lit up

by a moonless december night that might last
too long for stars to

keep their value, maybe some wizardry of
words will make a salve
for the wounds---maybe getting all hung up
on a cross with nails
of your own hammering is just the best you
can do---all you can do

to try to keep the spirits happy...to try to
dance away the fear---run up top the hill
to your own, makeshift cavalry---let the
trumpets blow, joshua, let it all blow down

## On the 3<sup>rd</sup> Day of Xmas

the building of walls was the first wave of
capture
the indirect assumption of power was more
crippling

than the great wars fought for so long
afterward
all in order to take down the walls, all in order
to

build more walls anew---to tower above the
last rampart
to obliterate the legend of the last power
struggle, as the fleas

& lice & the maggots never cheered us on, but
made a banquet
of our final love songs, wailed outward in
lament against stone

as we huddled behind structure, condemned
freedom as savage
unless it came with hegemony & validation of
form or practice

our love letters became txt messages, our
religions became
greeting cards, our hearts became commercial,
our wars
became so antiseptic we only watched what
we were told to

in blurred night vision on LCD screens while
characters you
could hardly make out in the digital fuzz made
out with our
last vestiges of love & freedom as we looked
at tiny phone

screens in numbed silences while another
holiday was being
prepared for another pre-planned celebration
of hollow dreams
along the wind blown scaffolds of all the
empty promises we celebrate alone

# On the 4<sup>th</sup> Day of Xmas

o tabernacle o tabernacle
the rings round the moon

o tabernacle o tabernacle
no sounds from the moor

o tabernacle o tabernacle
our heart beats too soon

o tabernacle o tabernacle
the cold numbs the hands

o tabernacle o tabernacle
looking for signs of you

o tabernacle o tabernacle
we know what we have done

but we don't know what to do

o tabernacle o tabernacle
your words fade to blue

like an old man's tattoo

o tabernacle o tabernacle
which way is love?

# On the 5<sup>th</sup> Day of Xmas

no savior ever was so docile
as the boy who walked
a mile-_-_-_to see the
girl in her happiest smile

she did not need to be
made to laugh__so much
as the boy, docile as any
savior might be, needed
to save her some laughter

o love is the way for them

these roads were built up now
paved with tears of those
who know no peace in sweet__
bethlehem, twain the steeple
twixt the dome or---upon the ground

o bethlehem

the rock that once was a wall
of a simple house that had
simpler rules so that we would be
saviors of ourselves__once

# On the 6<sup>th</sup> Day of Xmas

the children's choir
             sang---so clear/so bright
tonight in
        the homeless shelter
it was a
        moment__suspended---in time
as young
        voices held strong

as old hearts---sank deep__into
the mirth of the moment__the smiles

what can be will be in time__like
encyclopedias of emotions---flipping past

doing        somersault
    another        dance

on all these broken hearts

on all these mangled hearts

on all these brilliant hearts

as these voices blend & crack

*singing/singing/singing*

the harmonics of desperation

guiding the lost souls home__gifted

# On the 7<sup>th</sup> Day of Xmas

the beautiful hostage
god in gift wrapping
                    the torn whore
                    of cosmic
                    applause
take these wings
make for the
limelight__tonight
                    the flowers of winter
                     grow crystalline stems
among the presents
waiting for us all...
                    the world opens up
                    unwelcoming, like
                    raw oyster from a
     tainted seaside
                    no pearls---mystery
                    just another holiday
underneath all the
unnecessary parts
                    of an untold tragedy
                    that we all know by
                                   heart

# On the 8<sup>th</sup> Day of Xmas

there is shouting in the streets
injustices of air floating unseen

there is turmoil in the world, it
asks that we be reverent now

as the light is revealed above us
the talk in the dark is about past

ideas, before humanity looked to
sky gods, when the corporeal was

what we worshiped, not the surreal
abstractions of lights up high, im-

perceptable to the glass we had yet
to conceive of__only raindrops as

our convex of learning light refractions
as the trees grew up saintly, the rocks

held the souls of our ancient parents
& water was every where the spirit took us
inside & out

# On the 9<sup>th</sup> Day of Xmas

the mirage across the desert looks like a candelabra
turned upside down
sad clowns in the caravan don't want to watch the
road ahead too long

roadmaps__no one can find the way to a lost
civilization without one
the bones travel while we sleep, the mind travels
while the people talk

going away in one piece is the gift of the lonely magi,
crowned by hurt
water levels around the world ebb & flow to the
rhythm of it all the time

the lonely magi walks silently down the road, no one
notices, this is the way
nobody ever expects a tidal wave when they are
hoping for a savior's birth

even sad clowns are here to make us smile, quietly as
it is kept
even bones have to travel along the moonlit roadway
while we sleep

# On the 10<sup>th</sup> Day of Xmas

the tin soldiers gave way to rust
so long ago, replaced by the die cast
pot metal toys that were heavy as lead
which were countered by the aluminum
toys that were lighter but not as long
lasting as the new molded plastic
toys with rubberized skin &
silicon faces that hold
life-like eyes staring
back at you as if
to ask "what
future will
you make
for us
if we
promise
to live forever?"

# On the 11th Day of Xmas

listen to the big screen tv
glory to the show that sings

gather round ye' married men
rain dollars on the working girls

o little town of gun mayhem
may you always be well armed

single momma santa helper
powder bags & pill bottles

deck the hood in LED
convenience is not

apparently
the death
we once
thought
it to be

so feast
& be merry
ye gentlemen
of clubs & hearts
cum let us adore ye
cum let us abhor ye
o cum on festive asses
& faces that you desire

make no atonement in this time
of great spiritual might that smites
the weaker souls lost along the way

we kings we go assailing *we kings we go assailing*
from drones that sing on high, from angels of
random death that send out blessings down
upon the land of wisemen now burned

down to the ground

ground & pound the candy cane land
send the elves on reindeer hooves
watch the light shows as they
blink like stars obliterated
from chimney smoke
on cap & trade
corporate
power plant noels

reap this spirit shopping season
roast the chestnuts until they burn

the children that brought you all these possibilities
are just as happy as can be, working away in
workshops
with holly jolly snowmen guarding all the human
traffic
so the holidays can be happy for those that need them
most

# On the 12<sup>th</sup> Day of Xmas

baby jesus sits in the manger with all the adoration
he will never be an old man, walking down cold
streets

alone---no feast will be due father time in his passing
as he passes by baby jesus every year right after the

saturnalia__feasts of kings & virgin sacrifice, a child
is born
that might give hope to peace, but it still remains a
long shot

chance in a game of snowballs inside eternal inferno
where
everybody dances away to sounds of pitchfork
promises

told to children who need to be regulated---because
regulations
are what keep people in the seats__keep em paying
for the

dream---for the wonder of the pageantry__for the
secret
behind the mystery that never gets told as much as
the

fables told by shepherds that grow old & become
lonely
walking down streets mumbling something to
themselves...

(maybe about a star that was really a planet, but that
night...*you shoulda seen it*)

...then, mumbling something to
themselves__something that

nobody can hear over the canned music blaring from
the outdoor

speaker system some music designed by advertisers
to hypnotize
the shoppers into buying into it all a little more
deeply__praying for

                    a star

of their own someday in a sky full of planetary
mistaken identities
& legendary near misses that even father time can't
seem to calculate anymore

## Angels On High Greet the Shepherds Below

keep your song & dance up outta these old fields

more will get told,
                    so that more can be revealed

what mystery there must be
                        for a victory to be
                              sealed

the only opportunity right here
                        is for the__sick
                        to be healed

as the music keeps a playin'
                        the sound of it
                          is real

so listen to the angels, so high
                      they came to deal

## the birthdays, they come and go

it blows in on the wind, late at night, alone
stories they been told since before birth
about a lost virgin with no place to lay down
for a starry night in the desert land
across many seas, even more years ago

the real story is there in the books, plain as day
it was not the case, it was not even this time of year
a rabbi may have been born in that time, but
born a child of fornication, like all children are
he was born a boy, but grew into a man, a rabbi
a spiritual leader who viewed the status quo
as unjust and not spiritually fomenting to be love
a love that he saw so necessary in this world
from then on into the future, he saw the need for love
over all, over anything...love was god...god was good

his cries for justice caused a change that was powerful
it encompassed those outside his own religious tenets
it engulfed the minds, the hearts, even the souls
of many different lands, many different languages

then it became an arbitration of kingdoms on earth
as it sold space in an imaginary kingdom of heaven

it assimilated every spiritual belief that stood in the
way
of the rule of its ultimate law, the bearer of its
ultimate crown
the words of the rabbi who sought justice were
determined
to be only open for discussion at the feet

of mortal thrones
the dates of events would fit in with superseded
belief systems
celebrations took on new meaning with remnants
of ritual
leftover by whimsical tribes of the conquered subjects
and slaves

now it is the structure of commerce and patriots, bold
as they are
behind sophisticated weaponry and manufactured
rules of engagement
in wars they forge with the upheld throne of false
kingship hidden
behind flags and banners of conflicted democracy and
republic

onto this day, born into this world, a child came in
our time
a child that wanted nothing but history to be learned
well enough
so the lies that people were willing to die for
might be less lethal
than the truth they can't seem to live with
or the love they speak of, but deny when it is upon
them, so unjustly

May You Find All the Happiness You Seek

Made in the USA
Las Vegas, NV
31 October 2023